What to do
when your mom or dad says . . .
"DON'T OVERDO
WITH VIDEO GAMES!"

By
JOY WILT BERRY

Living Skills Press
Fallbrook, California

Distributed by:

Word, Incorporated
4800 W. Waco Drive
Waco, TX 76710

Dear Parent,

Are you growing increasingly concerned about your child's fascination with video games? If so, you have plenty of company. Many parents around the country are filled with doubts and questions about this new form of entertainment. They wonder whether the games are harmful, or even addictive. They worry about youngsters spending too much time and money on them. They worry about undesirable influences at video game rooms.

But while the worry goes on, so does the video game craze. New games are constantly being created for home and arcade use. It seems clear that these new "toys" are going to be around for a good long time. It seems equally clear that children are going to want to play them—because, quite simply, they're fun! And, used in the right way, they can be educational, not to mention helpful for coordination and muscle control.

That's the key phrase: *Used in the right way.* It isn't that video games in and of themselves are harmful. Problems arise instead when the attitudes, priorities, or habits of their users are out of line. That's why children must be encouraged to view video games in a balanced, reasonable way and to take the responsibility for their proper use. In other words, someone must tell them: **"DON'T OVERDO WITH VIDEO GAMES!"**

Children should be informed of these and other possible dangers of overdoing with video games:

- The games can provide an escape from problems and responsibilities.
- They can take the place of more creative amusements.
- Children can grow dependent on them for entertainment.
- The violence inherent in certain games may subtly encourage equally violent or destructive behavior.

Once children understand the dangers of overdoing with video games, they should learn how to bring their attraction under control. Then they can start assigning video games a reasonable place in their leisure time. As happens so often, once parameters are explained and set, the children will invariably be happier and more secure.

As for you, once you are comfortable that your child has this new amusement under control, you can relax a bit yourself. You might even find video games an enjoyable way to spend some time with your child. And you won't constantly have to warn: **"DON'T OVERDO WITH VIDEO GAMES!"**

Sincerely,

Joy Wilt Berry

4

Has your mom or dad ever told you:

Well, maybe they don't use those exact words. But when your parents warn you about video games, do you think . . .

If all this sounds familiar to you, you're going to **love** this book!

Because it will show you how to have the most fun with video games . . . and keep your parents happy too!

No matter who you are or where you live, chances are you play video games. If this is true, you are like many other people. Recent surveys show that more time is spent playing video games than playing anything else.

Playing video games is fun. But can playing video games hurt you?

Some parents, doctors, teachers and other concerned adults think that it can. Sometimes video games can provide an **escape from problems**. The games make it possible for people to run away from the things that are bothering them. Some people spend their time playing the games so that they will not have to face their problems.

Video games can also provide an **escape from responsibility**. The games encourage people to avoid doing the things they are supposed to do. Some people spend their time playing the games so that they will not have to work or do the things they do not want to do.

11

Too often video games can **take the place of friends and other people**. Some people choose to play video games over doing things with others. Unfortunately, they miss out on the wonderful experiences that are shared when people spend time together.

Video games can also **take the place of doing creative things**. People who spend all their free time playing the games may not have time to do other exciting things. Thus, they themselves may become dull and boring.

Video games may cause a person to **become dependent**. People who spend all their free time playing the games may begin to depend on the games for entertainment. They may not deal with their boredom in creative, productive ways. They might become very unhappy when there are no video games to occupy their time.

A person may **be dishonest** because of the video games. This can happen when the people who have become dependent on video games feel a need to play the games even when it is not best for them to do so. These people may lie to themselves or others in order to play the games.

A person may **spend too much money** on video games. Video games can cause people to play without realizing or caring how much money they are spending. These people keep putting money into the machines even when they should not be doing so. If they run out of money, they may steal so that they can continue to play the games.

Video games may cause a person to **become violent and perhaps even destructive.** This is because some of the video games subtly teach people that violence and destruction can lead to winning. They establish the winner as the one who destroys the most. Thus, destruction is shown to be an acceptable way to solve problems.

Obviously this is not good. Violence and destruction never solve anything. They only complicate situations and make things worse. Anything that encourages people to be violent or destructive is not good.

23

If it is true that video games may . . .

- provide an escape from problems,

- provide an escape from responsibility,

- take the place of friends and other people,

- take the place of doing creative things,

- cause a person to become dependent,

- cause a person to become dishonest,

- cause a person to spend too much money,

- cause a person to become aggressive and perhaps even violent,

. . . should anyone ever play video games? Should video games be banned? Should children be made to give them up?

Before you decide what should be done with video games, stop and think!

A video game is only an electrical machine. It cannot think. It cannot turn itself on or off.

But you can think, and you can turn a video game on and off.

You do not have to be controlled by a video game. Instead, you can and should control it.

Video games cannot hurt you if you control them and use them wisely.

In fact, a video game that is used properly can be a great source of fun and entertainment. It can also develop your hand/eye coordination.

It is not the video game that is good or bad; **it is the way you use the video game** that makes it good or bad.

29

There are several things that you must consider if you want to use video games properly.

They are . . .

- the **time** you spend playing the games,

- the **money** you spend playing the games,

- your **attitude** toward the games, and

- the **importance** you give to playing the games.

BLiPPP

WHAT'S A LITTLE TIME, OR MONEY?

The Time You Spend Playing the Games

Before you play a video game, you need to determine how much time you can spend playing it. Decide on a specific amount of playing time and **do not play more than that amount.**

Set a timer or ask another person to remind you when your playing time is up.

31

To help you decide upon a proper amount of playing time, you will need to determine how much free time you have.

Begin by thinking about a school day (or weekday). Consider the fact that there are 24 hours in a day. At least:

 8 hours are spent sleeping,
 1 hour is spent bathing, dressing and undressing,
 3 hours are spent eating and with family, and
 _8 hours are spent in and around school.
20 hours

If you subtract these 20 hours from the the total of 24 hours, you get a remainder of 4 hours. You must now subtract the time it takes to do your work and take care of home responsibilities. What you have left will be the free time you have each day during the week.

Next, figure out how much free time you have on the weekend. Remember to consider the time that is spent . . .

- in church or temple,

- doing chores, and

- participating in family and group activities.

Once you know how much free time you have, you can determine how much time you can spend playing the games. Do this by listing all of the things you need or want to accomplish during your free time. Decide how much time these things will take. Remember to include . . .

- activities with clubs and organizations,

- lessons,

- sports,

- playing with friends,

- watching TV, and

- hobbies.

Any remaining free time can be spent playing video games.

With everything life has to offer, it is likely that you are spending too much time on video games if you are spending more than twenty-five percent of your free time playing them.

35

The Money You Spend Playing the Games

Before you play a video game, you need to determine how much money you can spend playing it. Decide on a specific amount of money and **do not spend more than that amount.**

Do not go into a video game room carrying more money than you intend to spend. If you have an extra amount of money, ask a friend to hold it for you until you leave the video game room.

To help you decide how much money you can spend on video games, you will need to determine how much extra spending money you have.

Begin by listing your income. Your income is the money you expect to receive and includes your allowance and earnings.

Next, list your expenses. Your expenses are the monies you plan to spend and should include your savings, donations, needs and wants.

You will know how much extra spending money you have when you subtract your expenses from your income.

With all of the worthwhile things there are to spend money on, you are probably spending too much money on video games if you spend more than twenty percent of your total income on them.

Your Attitude Toward the Games

The purpose of games is to bring fun and relaxation into people's lives. Games that do not accomplish these things are pointless and should not be played.

If you experience fun and relaxation when you play video games, you might want to continue to play them. If on the other hand you become frustrated or upset when you play the games, you should stop playing them.

Any game, including a video game, should make you feel good, not bad. It should bring you joy, not sadness.

The most important part of any game is how you feel or what you experience while you are playing it. This is more important than whether you win or lose, or get a high score.

When you play a game to win with no concern about what happens to you while you are playing, you are missing the point of the game. This is what is meant by the saying, "It's not whether you win or lose, but how you play the game that counts."

If you find when you play video games that winning, or beating your previous high score, becomes more important than playing, you should not play them.

The Importance You Give to Playing the Games

The most important thing in your life is your survival and growth. Everything you do should contribute in one way or another to keeping you alive and to helping you become a healthy, productive person.

If video games keep you from doing the things that are good for you or if they hold back your growth in any way, you should not play them. In other words, you should stop playing the games if you spend so much time and energy playing them that you neglect your mental or emotional health.

The second most important thing in life is your relationship with other people. Doing things with others is important to your survival and growth.

If you are so busy playing video games that you are not spending time with other people, you should stop playing the games.

Thus, **you can make video games** a good or bad part of your life. It all depends on . . .

- how much time you spend playing the games,
- how much money you spend playing the games,
- your attitude toward the games, and
- the importance you give to playing the games.

Only you can **END** your mom or dad having to say, **"DON'T OVERDO WITH VIDEO GAMES!"**